If you pet a BBC, you'll be sure to shout boy, yippie!

But if you do dare consent to pet a BBC, you'll find it's not as easy as 1,2,3…

A BBC when wrangled right

won't scamper, recoil, shrink or bite!

If you've prepared mentally to pet a BBC

you won't dash away in fright at the first look-see!

Count with me!

"One-inch
two-inch
three-inch
four…

1
2
3
4
B
B
C

**Five-inch
six-inch
seven-inch**

Wait MORE?"

Oh, how far the inches can go…

Like a curbside weed, the BBC just grows and grows!

Where might you ask can one find a BBC?

Well, shucks… Down the street, at college or even under the park tree!

You're probably thinking wait a second Mam...

BBCs can be found in more than one place!

More than one country!

And even in cyberspace…

Hold your horses…

Or should I say hold your BBCs?

Yes, but also there are other subspecies like its cousin:

the BWC.

Let's save BBC family tree talk for another date and time…

Today's JUST about the BBC.

Now on to its venomous slime!

Careful now…

All it takes is one little dance with a BBC at a club.

All it takes is one picnic with a BBC for grub…

All it takes is for one BBC grooming in the tub…

And left you could be

with a BBC cub!

Now I've been called many things like…

Dummy, forgetful, thick and penny pincher…

But one thing's for certain…

Momma didn't raise no BBC flincher!

What I hope today you take away

that the BBC whether domestic or stray…

Is here to make one's day a little less gloomy!

But I hope for your sake, that you yourself, are roomy…

"Great, but who are you again Mam?

And, how do you know so much about BBCs?"

Oh, I'm just passing through…

but if you MUST know, I worked maintenance for a basketball arena…

I came face to face with BBCs MANY times on the job…

When groundskeeping…

When taking the trash out to the alley…

When cleaning the locker rooms…

You know, there was just something about them that filled that empty hole inside me…

But enough about Ol' Madge!

To find out how YOU can make a difference in a BBC's life…

Search BBC on Dad's computer and help GROW awareness!

Your contribution will go a LONG way!

Your smile will never have been so WIDE and so DEEP!

Oh, and don't mind when Dad finds out! His grumpiness will pass…

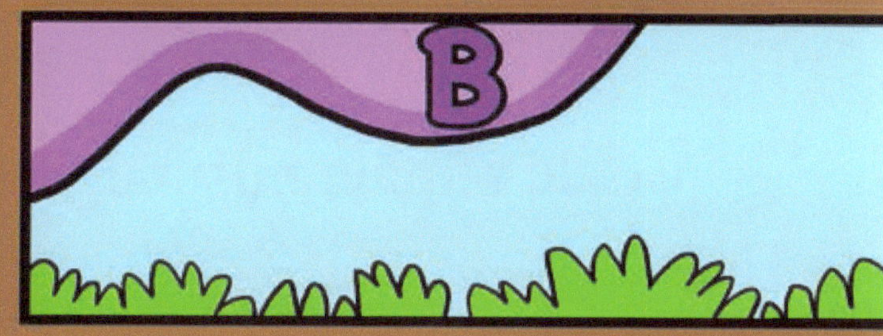

Dedicated to exotic animal caretakers.

Without people like you,

Big **B**oa **C**onstrictors

would remain misunderstood and feared.

If you suspect mistreatment of a **BBC** in your area, local and federal wildlife authorities are available to assist.

DON'T WAIT!

EVERY. SECOND. COUNTS.

<u>Some Facts About **Big Boa Constrictors!**</u>

Super sneaky hunters and quite powerful!

They can be found hunting at dark in Central and South America!

They pick up smells through their flickering tongues!

They can live for more than 20 years!

A female can have dozens of babies at a time!

They don't chew, they swallow prey whole!

Sometimes, they don't have to eat again for weeks if their meal is big enough!

A grown up can weigh more that 100 pounds!

They prefer to live alone, so don't bother them!

THE END!